THE GIFT OF FINDING GOD'S LOVE

Guilt and Shame Turned into My Shine

TENIECKA DRAKE

Copyright © 2018 Teniecka Drake
All rights reserved
First Edition

PAGE PUBLISHING, INC.
New York, NY

First originally published by Page Publishing, Inc. 2018

ISBN 978-1-64298-148-3 (Paperback)
ISBN 978-1-64298-149-0 (Digital)

Printed in the United States of America

CHAPTER 1

Domestic violence tends to be that shameful abuse that happens that nobody wants to talk about. For me, it was very difficult to acknowledge that I was in a domestically violent and extremely toxic relationship. Within this book, I am going to highlight different signs of cheating. Along with those signs will be helpful dos and don'ts for women to take note of. These are signs and lessons I learned from being involved in a domestically violent and abusive relationship. Throughout this book, I will share my story along with scriptures and ideas to meditate on. This book also has poems that capture some of the feelings surrounding my personal battle.

Although the experience I went through was traumatic, I found God and his love for me. I knew the Lord, having been raised in the church and having accepted Christ into my life at age seventeen. I rededicated my life to him again in my early twenties. As I embark upon this journey to share my story, it is all about God. God saw everything I was going through. Even though I wanted my marriage to work, I saw that my husband did not want the same. When you love someone, you do not want to hurt them. It is not the way love works. I found myself in a pattern of forgiving but it was toxic for me to stay. I have four beautiful children that the Lord has entrusted into my care. None of what they have witnessed was going to benefit them.

I kept forcing myself to stay and convincing myself that the Lord wanted me to stay. I had taken a covenant and oath to God. I was not about to just give up on this marriage. The truth of the matter is that this relationship was doomed from the start. The signs were there, but because I did not know what to look for, I started chalking those signs up to caring and loving gestures when they were exactly the complete opposite. One day, the Lord really had to take those rose-colored shades off. I recall telling one of my family members that I was waiting for him to show his true colors.

They said to me, "He has been showing you his true colors. What are you, color-blind?"

It was hard to hear, but that was the truth and could not be denied. I was actually the one in denial trying not to see what I was involved in. Let me not hold up any more of your time. I am going to just jump right in.

Cheating Signs You Do Not Ignore

1. *Anger*—if your significant other gets very angry discussing simple things.

    Example, you want to discuss bills or anything in general. The conversation turns into an argument.

2. *Irritability*—your significant other is always bothered by anything you do. All of a sudden, he does things that he would not normally do.

    Examples, gets a rental car, buys a new or luxury car that he never purchased before, has to go places all of a sudden.

3. *Secrecy*—secret texts, going on dating sites and posting "available," arranging meetings with other women and disguising them as "friendship."

Bonus Signs

- No longer wanting to be intimate.
- Pointing out physical attributes as major issues that were not before.
- For those either married or involved with a truck driver, taking longer truck trips and leaving sooner than normal.

The signs that have been mentioned are key. Now there are other variations to these. The best sign to look for is your gut—that female intuition. When you think or feel that something is not right, trust in it. Then you can watch, and sooner or later the truth will be exposed.

In a domestically violent relationship, cheating is part of the problem. On top of cheating is the denial and lying that there is no cheating happening. This person will, in fact, turns every single thing on you, trying to convince you that you are the one with the problem.

CHAPTER 2

The Do-Nots

God loves you so much. If you think or believe that you have to stay in an abusive relationship, I am here to tell you that you do not have to do that. Do not stay for your kids. This leads me into the do-nots in an abusive relationship.

God's Word Scripture Truth

Keep me safe, O God for in you I take refuge. I said to the Lord, "You are my Lord; apart from you I have no good thing." (Psalms 16:1–2)

Never rationalize staying in a toxic relationship.

There Are Nine Do-Nots
1. *Do not* believe the person will change.
2. *Do not* think you can change how that person acts.
3. *Do not* think it is your fault that your significant other hurts you.

4. *Do not* assume your significant other is not hurting them. Protect your kids.
5. *Do not* force yourself to stay after you realize you are in a toxic relationship. Leave your situation when it is safe to do so.
6. *Do not* think you cannot change where you are. Remember, you have the power to change your situation.
7. *Do not* think sorry means the abuse will stop. Even if it does, that is temporary no matter how long nothing occurs.
8. *Do not* ignore an aggressive temper, cuss words that are used to demean you, or any other form of disrespect.
9. *Do not* lie to yourself thinking your significant other has changed.

Do not associate jealousy, possessiveness, and controlling behavior for love. *It is not!*

Do not think that love is rude, nasty, mean, angry, threatening, or disrespectful.

Now that I have given you the do-nots, let us shift into what the good things to do are. These things-to-do will really open your eyes. Allow yourself to open up to receive assistance. You will be shocked to know that employers do care about employees being hurt. As bad as you may think your family might be, trust me when I say that your family cares and they will open their doors for their family member. Remember that nobody can help you if you do not speak up and speak out. What do you need to know in order to have the support you need?

God's Word Scripture Truth

> *In my distress I called to the Lord; I cried to my God for help. From his temple he heard my voice; my cry came before him, into his ears.* (Psalms 18:6)

God will use your life and your situation as a testimony to his glory.

God never gives us more than we can bear. You may not see it now but God has already removed you from that toxic environment. Start to visualize a day of peace. A day with no arguing and yelling back and forth. Visualize your happiness and freedom and no one having control over you. Visualize your children, happy and not afraid or jumpy. Let's get into some dos that will be very helpful to you. They were for me as I truly realized the power I had.

CHAPTER 3

The Dos

There Are Eleven Helpful Dos

1. *Do* prepare in your mind a worst-case scenario and plan for it.
2. *Do* let law enforcement be aware of the situation and start reporting the incidents. You will start getting incident reports as proof there has been domestic violence. That will become a record and log for you.
3. *Do* let family and friends that you trust know about your situation. (Unveil who this monster truly is.)
4. *Do* know you are none of the evil names, gestures, disrespectful, mean, and nasty things that your significant other calls you.
5. *Do* know you are strong when you survive abuse from your abuser.
6. *Do* understand that you do not deserve to be treated poorly or hit on, ever.

7. *Do* know your worth, women and men. A person that has to resort to hitting is trying to control you.
8. *Do* know that they cannot control you unless you let yourself be controlled.
9. *Do* let your employer know, if you are employed. (You will be surprised how employers are ready to help a valuable employee.)
10. *Do* remember to enjoy life.
11. *Do* remember to do hobbies crafts, sports, or anything you may have stopped due to this person's behavior.

Trust that God will repay. "Vengeance is mine," thus says the Lord.

CHAPTER 4

My Story

I am going to share my story about surviving domestic violence. It has been a long road. I am a survivor and overcomer of domestic violence.

Being married to my husband was extremely rough. I got married on May 27, 2008. My daughter was born in June on the 13th of 2008. On July 4, 2008, my husband and I had gotten into an argument. Ask me now and I cannot recall why, only because it must have been petty. He punched a hole on the bedroom door. He hit me for some reason. I went into the garage of the house with our daughter who was only a month old then. I cried and cried in the dark garage while watching the fireworks.

After the first incident, the hitting, throwing, and mental abuse became more frequent. He could go for four months or two months without hitting or shoving. Then something I say or do would provoke him or set him off. It was the same story. "Baby, I am sorry. You know I love you. I am going to change starting today."

Every day since then, he kept repeating that phrase. Until our eighth year of marriage. Then he would say, "I know you hear this all the time but I really am going to change."

Within my marriage, I have done some horrific things due to my husband's influence. Of course, I take responsibility for allowing myself to be persuaded. It sickens me that I have even cheated on him so he would divorce me. I was tired of the abuse, the negative, degrading talk, and the mentally insulting names. Even the dangerous ways he had. Here is a poem that I wrote as I sat and thought about what I noticed about my spouse.

The Abuser

You were so loving and charming. Then you started to do things that were alarming. I thought, it is okay, it will get better another day. One day turned to a week, a week into a month. A month into years. Then what do I have to fear? "It will get better," I convinced myself. I know it will. You promise, "I will stop today." *Smack!* "Oh, baby, I am sorry, I love you." You would woo me back with your charms. What charms can come from you, what harms? The abuser wants to keep you trapped. Now you have awoken from the haze of toxic love. Today you say, "No more today." The abuser has no more power over you. You have now said "No more," not today or any other day!

Sometimes, it is not so easy to leave a toxic relationship. He always wanted to know where I was. To play if off he would say, "I don't care where you go."

I knew that was a lie. I was a stay-at-home mother during all of this. I even got my bachelor's while pregnant, and dealing with and providing for him. We were living on one income at that time. He was not able to work due to child support. We lived on $123 a month. It was only by the grace of God that we made it. He had not been working for almost five years. I supported our entire family.

All those years went by and in 2015, I told him I was going to try out for this state job. God was in all of this. He was keeping me and watching over me and my children. I had found this job through the church I was attending at that time. The church, Salvation Army, was very supportive during all this. They would continuously pray for me. I got the state job in September of 2015. I loved it because it was a career. It was allowing me to be independent again. I was surrounded by strong women who happened to be women of faith. The state job found out about my situation and moved me to another location.

Since my husband was a truck driver, he did not know I was moved. He kept staying out longer and longer due to him finding another love interest.

In April 2016 I had really started planning in my head how I was going to leave him. My family had even been helping put myself and the kids in hotels because he had shut the water off on us. He had also cut the electricity off. During the summer in Arizona, it is too hot not to have air-conditioning.

When I really made up my mind to leave, a very small voice told me, "You need to leave now! You need to pack up and go!"

At that time, I was living in a hotel due to the electricity being cut off again, and my husband not wanting to pay the bill. He had come back from his truck trip and had seen the hotel where we were staying. He then said he had to leave again, which I did not care about. I was ready.

My management team and HR understood that I had to leave. They were all so supportive. I recall my manager saying, "Sometimes you have to go back in order to move forward."

My supervisor stated, "I am a big advocate of family. Definitely go back to your family."

I made sure I got rid of the trash, packed up the kids, and left Arizona. I had never traveled so far alone before, on the interstate. Here I was, a mother with all her belongings she could take, and four kids. We made a six-hour drive. I left at 3:00 p.m. and arrived at midnight in California. Needless to say, the story is not over yet. God is still working it out for me and my children. I am still currently married to him, although I have moved. He has now moved to California as well.

God's Word Scripture Truth

For the Lord loves justice and does not forsake his godly ones; They are preserved forever. (Psalm 37:28)

All I know is that my life is starting over. God brought me to this point for his glory. My story will be a true testimony to God working it out. Prayer changes things. It is all about having faith in him. God has been telling me to leave. I ignored the signs and warnings. After finally listening and being obedient to his Word and his voice, he did remove me out of my toxic relationship. I am changing and becoming stronger every day.

Lord, thank you for always protecting me and my children. God, you are so good and worthy of my praise!

It is time for women to THINK—meaning, The Hurt Is Now Knowledge. If you think long and hard and watch, your aggressor has a pattern. At times, especially in the beginning stages you cannot tell. I started to see that my husband had many patterns. One example of a pattern is if he wanted something from me. He would be very nice, very charming, and extremely apologetic. I had to THINK why that was. He was playing on how I operated. We do not understand that an aggressor/abuser is a predator. He or she studies your personality. He learns how far he can push you. After a while, when you get sick and tired, you notice the pattern. Some aggressors are not willing to change. They will do the same thing they did in a previous relationship. Since they do not want to truly change, they just remain the same. What is it like to carry around pain as a wife struggling through domestic violence? I have a poem that touches on the pains of a wife.

A Wife's Pain

The expectation of a wife I never knew. I believed a wife, cooking and cleaning is all she had to do. A wife's pain takes more burdens than she can bear. Keeping the kids clean and making their rooms. I assumed there was more to do without a broom. A wife's pain takes more burdens than she can bear. Am I to believe that a duty of a wife is to surrender her rights? The husband makes rules she must follow, is that right? She is to be his sexual muse whenever he pleases. She should be able to be his emotional garbage can whenever it suits him. The wife must remain attractive, have no opinions, and should not be disrespectful and tend to everyone's needs. A wife's pain takes more burdens than she can bear. Why do you cry, wife? Your tears do not move anyone to care. You are not worthy of empathy or sympathy. Your story is a made-up lie you tell for a pity party. A wife's pain takes more burdens than she can bear. I suffered in silence. I suffered in shame. Though this, one fact remains. Jesus was there through every tear. Jesus was there through every blow. Jesus was there through you being called all those terrible names. A wife's pain takes more than she can bear. Jesus said, "My child, don't you see? The burdens you bore are for me. Cast your cares on me because a wife's pain and burdens you will bear no more.

In these very controlling and toxic relationships, we stay for many reasons. There are three reasons why I convinced myself to stay:

1. *God's covenant*—marriage
    I told myself, "God, I cannot break your covenant. I know my faith is so important."

2. *Two-parent household*—stability for my children to have both parents in the home.
    I did not want my kids growing up in a broken home. I just kept wanting to fight for a marriage that was toxic.

3. *The children*—they love their dad.
    I wanted to stay for the children's sake. As long as I kept trying and praying, I figured it just had to get better. Nothing I did or said changed his behavior toward myself or the children.

Reality check—God wants you to be happy. Why would he want his child to be hurt on a regular basis?

The answer to that is, he does not want that. God loves you and me so much that he sent his Son to die for us. He wants us to have peace. God created the institution of marriage for good reasons. The husband is ultimately supposed to love, honor, respect, protect, and provide for the wife. Anything contrary to loving and honoring her is not what God would want for marriage. In Hebrews 13:4, it says, *"Marriage is to be held in honor among all, and the marriage bed is to be undefiled; for fornicators and adulterers God will judge."*

At times all throughout my marriage, I wondered what I was doing with this man. I cried out so many times to God to help me. Oftentimes, God gives us signs or speaks to us. Instead of being quiet and listening out for his voice, we miss him speaking and the signs he sends. I sought God long and hard. I knew he was there, but I really was hearing myself complain and having a pity party for myself. The day God snapped me out of my foggy haze of confusion, everything got clear real quick. I had this sense of urgency to move.

When you feel in your spirit something's not right, that is the Holy Spirit speaking. The voice is quiet, but in that moment you know that it is time to get into action. After all the trying experiences I went through, I survived it all. I am here today to share so that somebody will be encouraged by it. I have written a poem addressing my survival.

I Survived I Am Alive

I survived I am alive. You thought I would not go because I loved you so. I survived I am alive. Truth be told I always wanted to go. I survived I am alive. My children watched how you hurt me time and time again. I survived I am alive. You said I am too ugly to find anybody else. I survived I am alive. You said you loved me and found others to love as well. I survived I am alive. I never knew I could be raped by a person I trusted. I survived I am alive. You choked me in an attempt to stop my life. I survived I am alive. God has kept me all these years. He will continue to keep me. I am no longer afraid because I survived I am very alive.

When you trust God, he will work it out for you. It may not be as quickly as you want it to be. It is good to remember that his timing is perfect.

CHAPTER 5

The Transition Period: Waiting and Watering Season

I gave some of my story to show how God moves and provides. In this section, I will be discussing the transition, otherwise known as the waiting and watering season. After leaving that situation, I moved in with my parents again. I had been gone only for ten years. Family tends to have a different dynamic. My initial intentions when I arrived was to hurry up and find a place. I would search online or drive around just searching. Housing was on the very top of my list. I knew my family was a lot to handle. I have four children and two of them receive assistance due to learning delays. On January 2016, I found out that one of my daughters is autistic. At the same time, my youngest has a global speech delay. Both children are not able to express any needs very clearly. Why am I mentioning this about my children? It will help give you a sense of the challenges I faced, but I still found the courage to leave. God gave me courage to remove myself.

God's Word Scripture Truth

Have I not commanded you? Be strong and courageous. Do not be terrified; do not be discouraged, for the Lord your God will be with you wherever you go. (Joshua 1:9)

Now back to the transition period. When I arrived at my parents', I assumed I would be gone. I had a timeframe of about three to four months. I was wrong. It became very clear to me that housing would be my biggest hurdle. At times, I did not understand why God had these things happen to me. When this particular thought came to me, I had to capture it. I think of the many times God had given me a way to leave, but due to my stubbornness, I did not heed the Lord's signs. During this transition, I have decided to really embrace God's Word. This transition period equates to being a waiting and watering season. Seeking God is what has kept me grounded and focused.

God's Word Scripture Truth

Ask and it will be given to you, seek and you will find, knock and the door will be opened to you. For everyone who asks receives; he who seeks finds; and to him who knocks, the door will be opened to you. (Matthew 6:7–8)

While I was seeking him and getting into the Word, God showed me his love. He gave me the gift by showing how much he truly loves and cares for me. The season of waiting and watering helped me to discover God like never before. The only way I did this was by spending time on his Word. I had to know that the God I serve is not sleeping. It was like he was telling me, "Daughter, listen to me."

As I listened, I trusted, not even certain of what would happen. God always has a plan for us. What we have to start believing about God is that, he's got our back. We can leave everything and say, "Lord, I do not know how this will work but I trust you."

When we do that, God moves for us. Blessings start to flow and he shows us strength. That is the gift of finding God's love. While being in the season of waiting and watering, God allows us to just wait for him. He will work it all out but we have to be willing to surrender to him completely.

God's Word Scripture Truth

> *I have been crucified with Christ and I no longer live in the body. I live by faith in the Son of God who loved me and gave himself for me.* (Galatians 2:20)

In the midst of the storm, God wants us to keep our eyes stayed on him. The enemy will throw storms and in the midst of the storm, we have to stop looking at our situations. When we really trust God, we know he is going to fix the situation or circumstance. The enemy causes these storms because he wants to distract you.

My storms were merely a distraction. Not only was the enemy trying to bind me physically and emotionally, but spiritually as well. I was literally in a fight or argument just to worship the Lord. I would not be able to go to church without an argument. God saw it all and removed me out of a chaotic situation.

When the storms of life come against you, stand firm in Jesus. When adversity rears their nasty heads of despair, hopelessness, fear, and doubt, you stand on the promises of God. When everything around you is uncertain and you do not know how it is all going to work out, you hold on to God's unchanging Word. God will never leave you no matter how difficult. God is yet working out your situation. What do you do in the meantime, while you are going through these storms in life? The first thing you need to do is pray about it all the time. Secondly, get your sword which is the Word of God and get it into your spirit. Third, have faith. Believe and act by trusting God. Go with the expectation that he has already worked it out. When you have done all you can do, let God have his way. Surrender it all to him, and he will not fail you.

Reflecting on Inward Change

My story about domestic violence has been difficult and now I am reflecting back on it. Even through all this trauma, God shows his love. Now the big storm has passed and the sun has come out in my life. I have been blessed to be in a church where I share crafting. Crafting for me, was a huge coping mechanism. I had never truly realized how powerful it was. Crafting and creating beautiful things kept me safe. You may ask, how were you safe? Every time I would craft, the husband would never bother me. In fact, it was almost a way of having peace and calm. Now, I look to my crafting for peace, happiness, calm, and safety. Crafting helps me to relax and really be involved in the process of creating. Since the abuse I have been involved in a DV and anger management group. I have also been doing individual therapy. The children have been receiving individual therapy as well. I realize that this is a process and will not be resolved overnight. After all that I have gone through, I can still say, "Praise God."

I am speaking up to acknowledge myself and give a voice to not only for me but for others. It does not matter if you are a man or a woman. The bottom line is, nobody deserves to be hurt in any form or fashion. What are some of these abuses?

- emotional abuse
- verbal abuse
- mental abuse
- physical abuse
- spiritual abuse
- digital abuse

These abuses are all different. Physical abuse is usually the type people notice as the most obvious. The other ones are just as bad, sometimes worse. They are all forms of control and trying to make the other person do as he or she is told.

When I think about all of these, can I truly say I was loved? My answer to that is no. I see I was never loved. I wanted to think I was doing something wrong. It was not me at all. It was the other person not wanting to stop those toxic behaviors. People can show you if they love you by how much they are willing to change to be with you. Many doctors and therapists all echoed the same thing to me. If that person does not value you as a person, they do not need to be with you. My self-esteem had taken a hit as I found myself second-guessing decisions. A spiral of unending thoughts flooded my mind like rushing water from the oceans tides. I wondered if I will ever find real true love again. Knowing how much my Heavenly Father loves me, I know there has to be a man he has designed just for me. I keep faith and hope in my heart that one day, I may know love real love again. I truly love my children and I never want them to ever feel that loss of love.

Can these thoughts I have truly be changed?

I knew my thoughts needed to change. The longer I sat with negative thoughts, the more I wanted to believe them. After going to these groups and therapies, I reflected on what I was doing. I had time to reflect back on the things I suffered through and endured to keep my sanity, and to look at where I had come from. Even more so, where God had brought me from. I can say unequivocally and unapologetically that he brought me out of that. It took all that I had to muster up the strength and the courage to make that move. Many people during this process asked me why I did not leave sooner. After being out of it, I started to question myself, like, "Yeah, how come I did not leave sooner?" I was reminded so many times that my body was on survival mode. It was busy keeping me safe and alert. All my senses were heightened and I was always ready to run. I had recently learned about the body's primitive instincts. They are the three natural responses of fight, flight, or freeze. I found that my response was flight. I knew leaving was the best choice.

Now that I did, I can look back and say I made the right choice leaving. Staying would have caused my body more harm than good.

THE GIFT OF FINDING GOD'S LOVE

Since I made all these changes, I am truly happy. I am looking forward to a great future. If you are in a domestically violent relationship, let the people you trust know. God will bring you out.

About the Author

Teniecka Drake is a veteran of the United States Air Force. Teniecka Drake has been a public speaker in the past. She is also a blogger for Thebody.com. She has been in the national magazine, "Ebony 2011" issue. She is also included in the Anthology titled, "Sistah's Speak." She does crafting classes at her church. This is her very first book sharing about herself. She believes that laughter is always the best medicine. She lives in California with her four beautiful children.

www.ingramcontent.com/pod-product-compliance
Lightning Source LLC
LaVergne TN
LVHW091935070526
838200LV00068B/1282